# *The Little Black & White Book of Life*

***A Guide to a Healthy and Purpose Driven Life***

***Anna***

ISBN:

# Table of Contents

# Dedication

*This book is dedicated to my incredible family and friends. May these words serve as a tribute to appreciate and accept the valuable lessons that have enriched our lives.*

*To my dear family, your constant presence has been a source of inspiration and a testament to the power of love and connection that has shaped me. The support I receive from you all is one of the greatest gifts in my life.*

*To Melissa, thank you for being a friend who has journeyed with me through life with unconditional love and acceptance. Together, we have shared laughter, tears, dreams, and aspirations. Your friendship has been a true source of comfort and growth.*

*To Grant, thank you for supporting me in every thing I do. Your loyalty, strength, and discipline is something I can count on everyday. I am so grateful to have you in my life.*

*With heartfelt appreciation,*
*Anna Caitlyn*

# About the Author

Anna Caitlyn is a renowned health coach specializing in supporting high performers in their respective fields. With a comprehensive background in integrative medicine from Duke University and certifications as a health coach, yoga teacher, and meditation expert, Anna brings a wealth of knowledge and experience to her practice. Her mission is to help individuals feel their best and achieve their peak goals by taking a holistic, whole-person approach. By combining her expertise in communication and human sciences with her deep understanding of behavior change, Anna empowers her clients to discover new levels of clarity and fulfillment. Her unique blend of skills and dedication makes her a trusted guide on the journey toward optimal health and well-being.

Healthbyac.com

*You are holding a cup of coffee when someone comes along and bumps into you or*

*shakes your arm, making you spill your coffee everywhere.*

*Why did you spill the coffee?*

*"Because someone bumped into me!!!"*

*Wrong answer.*

*You spilled the coffee because there was coffee in your cup.*

*Had there been tea in the cup, you would have spilled tea.*

*Whatever is inside the cup is what will spill out.*

*Therefore, when life comes along and shakes you (which WILL happen), whatever is inside you will come out.*

*It's easy to fake it until you get rattled.*

*So, we must ask ourselves… "what's in my cup?"*

*When life gets tough, what spills over?*

*Joy, gratefulness, peace, and humility?*

*Anger, bitterness, harsh words, and reactions?*

*Life provides the cup; YOU choose how to fill it.*

- Unknown

# Preface

This book is designed to be flexible in its reading approach, accommodating readers who prefer to read it cover to cover as well as those who prefer to open it to any chapter that resonates with them at the moment. It caters to individual preferences and needs, encouraging readers to explore the chapters that call out to them or address specific areas of interest or concern. Whether readers choose a linear reading experience or a more intuitive, non-linear approach, the book strives to provide valuable insights and guidance for personal growth and self-reflection.

You can expect practical advice, strategies, and insights to help cultivate a balanced and fulfilling lifestyle. This guide delves into various aspects of well-being, including physical, mental, and emotional health, as well as personal growth, relationships, and finding one's true purpose. It provides a roadmap for creating positive habits, setting meaningful goals, and developing a mindset that fosters resilience, mindfulness, and self-compassion. With actionable steps and inspiring perspectives, this guide empowers individuals to make conscious choices, nurture their well-being, and live a life aligned with their values and passions. Whether seeking guidance on nutrition, exercise, stress management, goal-setting, or finding meaning in everyday life, this guide offers valuable insights and practical tools for creating a healthy and purpose driven life.

# Chapter 1: Get Mentally Prepared

*"The unexamined life is not worth living."*

- Plato

In this book, we will embark on a journey toward greater happiness, health, and clarity. To ensure a transformative experience, it is crucial, to be honest with yourself and establish a few key concepts. Let's explore these concepts to align our understanding.

A key concept is the importance of spending time alone with your thoughts. True alone time means being present with your thoughts and not being distracted by your phone or other forms of entertainment. It is in these moments of solitude that great ideas and personal growth can flourish. Nikola Tesla and Isaac

Newton are examples of individuals who made significant discoveries while being alone with their thoughts. Embracing solitude and becoming comfortable with your own thoughts will give you a genuine advantage over others and place you ahead of the majority. It's important to note that being busy should not be seen as a badge of honor but rather as a sign of poor time management and an overused excuse.

We will also delve into the process of generating good ideas. I'm telling you how to do this now so that you can attribute all your future good ideas to reading this book. Contrary to popular belief, good ideas often arise when you release the active pursuit of them. By observing with curiosity and avoiding black-and-white thinking, you create space for remarkable ideas to develop. Many people find discomfort in the realm of the unknown, preventing them from allowing extraordinary possibilities to manifest. It's essential to embrace uncertainty and suspend judgment, as this can transform a good idea into a truly exceptional one. All your dreams are waiting in the realm of the unknown, and by creating space and opportunity, you can turn those dreams into reality.

Another notion to understand is the power of compounding interest, what I consider the 8th wonder of the world. If you have found something you're truly passionate about, give it one more month, one more year. When Warren Buffett was 30, he had 1 million dollars. By the time he reached his 50s, he had around $300 million. In his mid-60s, his net worth reached $16.5 billion, and in his 70s, it climbed to $35.7 billion. The difference between a million and a billion is substantial, and those additional years make an enormous difference. However, it's also important to acknowledge the value of “failing fast.” This skill comes from cultivating your intuition and regulating your ego so that you know when to persist or let go. Additionally, it's crucial to understand that compounding anything is neutral until expressed. You can spiral downward, just as you can spiral upward. Both paths will compound. That's why you might wake up one day and realize, "Oops, I've gained 15 pounds." But if you've experienced that, you also know that you can spiral in the opposite direction.

Since you're reading this book, I want to congratulate you because you are spiraling upward. Stay the course, and you will witness results.

Beware, immediate results are not always guaranteed, as I've experienced personally through practicing meditation and gratitude. Persisting in these practices eventually led to experiencing new levels of inner peace and joy, but it took time. Many people give up before reaping the benefits, but by persisting, you can achieve deep inner peace and fulfillment. This book is designed to provide you with information, philosophies, and actionable steps to cultivate these positive experiences in your own life. Reflecting on your progress, you may find yourself ten times happier than before, regardless of external circumstances.

Keep in mind acting from your most authentic self is crucial for significant progress. Shedding "safety shields" and learned behaviors that keep you from being fully authentic is essential. It can be scary to be yourself in a world where cancellation and rejection are prevalent, but it's time to embrace your true self. Losing relationships or jobs that don't align with your authentic self is a necessary step towards finding people and situations that appreciate the real you. This book encourages you to celebrate and accept who you are at your core. Meditation is a powerful tool to cut through the noise and connect with your true self in a loving and compassionate space. As you peel back the layers and embrace your authenticity, clarity will emerge, and life will start to make more sense. The journey to self-discovery may involve growing pains and losses, but the comfort and inner peace that come from acting from your core are worth it. Your authenticity will be a breath of fresh air not only to yourself but also to everyone around you.

Lastly, a good night's sleep has the power to answer many of life's questions. If you don't prioritize your sleep, you're making a rookie mistake. At least while you're reading this book, prioritize sleep hygiene.

# Chapter 2: Doing Your Best and Letting Go of the Rest

*"Happiness is not something ready-made. It comes from your own actions."*

- Dalai Lama

Self-doubt is a common hurdle for many people, but it can be detrimental to our well-being and progress. It keeps us trapped in negative thoughts and feelings, hindering us from reaching our full potential. However, by learning to do our best and letting go of self-doubt, we can enhance our mental and emotional health and achieve our goals.

Contrary to popular belief, doubting yourself doesn't lead to greater productivity or success. Instead, approaching ourselves with love and confidence allows us to foster growth and positive change. Many believe that self-criticism and doubt drive productivity, but the opposite is true. Through self-compassion and trust, we can nurture ourselves and create environments that support our development. We accomplish this by taking care of our physical and mental well-being, cultivating healthy relationships, and making choices that align with our values.

While some may have achieved success driven by fear or insecurity, true fulfillment comes from self-belief and inner peace. Merely chasing external achievements tends to leave us unsatisfied, forever yearning for more. The path to success and happiness lies in self-assurance, where setting boundaries, pursuing goals, and maintaining balance is essential.

A crucial aspect of personal growth is letting go of doubt and committing to doing our best. By focusing on doing our best rather than striving for perfection, we liberate ourselves from the chains of judgment. Setting realistic and achievable goals allows us to make progress and grow without falling into the destructive cycle of doubt.

Furthermore, letting go of self-doubt requires cultivating kindness and compassion toward ourselves. Self-doubt often stems from a lack of self-acceptance and forgiveness. By embracing kindness and compassion, we learn to accept our mistakes, learn from them, and move forward without dwelling on them.

Forgiveness is also essential in letting go of self-doubt. Holding onto resentment and refusing to forgive burdens us with negativity. As the saying goes, "Resentment is like drinking poison and expecting the other person to die." By practicing forgiveness towards ourselves and others, we lighten our emotional load and create space for self-compassion and personal growth.

It is crucial to notice and acknowledge when we engage in self-doubt and understand its underlying causes. Doubt often arises from past experiences, ingrained beliefs, or the influence of significant people in our lives. By recognizing the root, we can work on changing our thought patterns and letting go of judgment.

Finally, self-doubt often poses a significant hurdle that can hinder our well-being and progress. By embracing the understanding that our best is fluid and letting go of doubt, we can improve our mental and emotional health and achieve our goals. True happiness and fulfillment come from our own actions and the belief and confidence we have in ourselves. Trusting ourselves is a powerful catalyst for personal growth and success.

# Chapter 3: Don't Overlook Trust

*"Whoever is careless with the truth in small matters cannot be trusted with important matters."*

- Albert Einstein

Trusting ourselves is essential for living a fulfilling and successful life. When we have self-trust, we gain the confidence to make decisions and pursue our goals with determination. However, trusting oneself can be a challenging and ongoing process. It begins with a simple yet crucial realization: in order to trust ourselves, we must prioritize self-care.

Self-care is crucial for building self-trust. By taking care of ourselves, we demonstrate that we are deserving of love and care. This can involve activities such as exercise, healthy eating, and ensuring an adequate amount of sleep. Additionally, self-care encompasses practices like therapy, journaling, and spending time in nature. These activities not only enhance our physical well-being but also contribute to building self-esteem and fostering confidence in ourselves.

Another significant aspect of self-trust is following through on the promises we make to ourselves. When we fail to honor these commitments, it becomes easy to fall into a pattern of self-doubt and mistrust. Just as a friend wouldn't trust us if we repeatedly broke promises to meet them for lunch, neglecting our commitments to ourselves erodes our self-trust. It is important to recognize the impact of these broken promises, even small ones like hitting the snooze button, as they can undermine our self-trust. Therefore, setting realistic goals that we can genuinely follow through with is crucial.

Self-trust creates a sense of comfort in the world around us. It diminishes self-doubt and encourages us to take decisive action. Furthermore, self-trust aligns our decision-making with our core values and beliefs, enabling us to stay true to ourselves.

It is worth noting that building self-trust often involves engaging in activities that may not immediately bring joy. Some actions may feel pleasurable at the moment but lead to negative consequences, such as excessive drinking or reconnecting with an ex-partner. On the other hand, certain activities may feel challenging or uncomfortable initially, like holding a plank or starting a meditation practice. However, we can consciously choose to align our actions with our values, overriding the default feelings associated with certain actions. Additionally, once we develop good habits, we tend to enjoy and continue them. Since our lives are predominantly shaped by our habits, it is essential to cultivate positive ones, as both positive and negative habits become ingrained with time.

Trusting ourselves is vital for a fulfilling and successful life. Practicing self-care and honoring the promises we make to ourselves are essential steps in building self-trust. By trusting ourselves, we enhance our comfort in the world, take decisive actions aligned with our goals, and remain true to our values.

# Chapter 4: Taking Action

## *The Importance of Starting and Letting Go of Perfection*

*"Don't hope it's not cold. Put on a jacket and go outside anyways."*

- Shane Parrish

Taking action is a crucial step in achieving our goals and creating the life we desire. However, many of us get caught up in planning, preparing, and seeking perfection, which prevents us from taking the first step. It's essential to recognize that taking action and getting started is more valuable than striving for perfection.

Moreover, it's important to refrain from squelching someone else's hope. We often encounter situations where we dismiss others' ideas or dreams, thinking they won't work or won't be successful. However, we should avoid dampening their spirits. History has shown countless examples of seemingly absurd ideas that eventually succeeded. We all have different life experiences, and failure can be an invaluable teacher. It's crucial to allow ourselves and those around us the freedom to fail and learn from their experiences.

Fear of failure is one of the primary reasons why we often hold back from taking action. We worry about the possibility of not succeeding or making mistakes. Yet, failure is an intrinsic part of the learning process. Each failure presents an opportunity for growth and learning. By embracing failure as a natural part of the journey, we can overcome our fear and take action toward our goals.

Fear of the unknown can also hinder our progress. We may find ourselves anxious about what the future holds and the potential outcomes if we take that initial step. However, it's crucial to acknowledge that we can't predict or control everything that lies ahead. By letting go of the fear of the unknown, we open ourselves up to new possibilities and experiences.

Indecision can be a formidable hindrance to personal growth. When we find ourselves unable to make clear and decisive choices, we become trapped in a state of uncertainty and stagnation. Indecision prevents us from taking necessary risks, exploring new opportunities, and fully committing to our goals and aspirations. It keeps us in a perpetual state of doubt, fear, and hesitation, hindering our progress and limiting our potential. The inability to make decisions can lead to missed opportunities and a lack of forward momentum. Growth requires stepping outside of our comfort zones, embracing change, and making choices that align with our values and aspirations. By overcoming indecision and embracing a proactive mindset, we open ourselves up to new experiences, learning opportunities, and personal development. Making choices, even if they are not always perfect, allows us to learn, grow, and move forward on our journey toward self-improvement and fulfillment.

Additionally, the fear of not being perfect often acts as a roadblock on our journey toward success. We worry that our work won't be good enough or that we'll make mistakes. However, perfection is an unattainable standard, and as humans, we are inherently fallible. By releasing the need for perfection and embracing imperfection, we can take action and begin working towards our goals.

Taking action is essential for progress and personal growth. It's crucial to prioritize getting started over striving for perfection. We should avoid stifling others' hope and allow ourselves and those around us the freedom to fail and learn from their experiences. By embracing failure, letting go of the fear of the unknown, and releasing the need for perfection, we can take meaningful action and make significant strides toward achieving our goals. Progress is more important than perfection, and the journey begins with that first step.

# Chapter 5: Fitness

## Achieving Optimal Health

*"For he who has health has hope, and he who has hope, has everything."*

- Owen Arthur

Achieving optimal health requires prioritizing various aspects of our lifestyle. One of the most crucial factors is sleep. Prioritizing sleep is essential for overall health, especially cognitive well-being. Numerous studies support the importance of adequate sleep in feeling good and maintaining mental sharpness. Before embarking on a workout routine or dieting, it's crucial to address any sleep issues.

Nutrition plays a significant role in our health as well. While it's true that you can't outwork a bad diet, even those who can eat anything without gaining body fat should pay attention to what they consume. Our dietary choices influence not only our body composition but also our longevity, mood, and brain health. There's a reason many Billionaires invest in biotech companies because once you have every resource, you realize the undeniable truth that healthspan and lifespan are two very different things. It's important to remember that without good health, it's challenging to truly enjoy life.

Many people strive to sustain peak performance throughout the day without encountering energy slumps. While individual nuances may vary, a few general strategies can help us feel good and avoid brain fog by making mindful dietary choices. Firstly, portion control is crucial. Consuming large meals can divert blood flow away from the brain, hindering cognitive function, particularly during important tasks like presentations.

Intermittent fasting can be beneficial for autophagy, simplifying meal planning, and supporting weight management. However, it's important to note that premenopausal women should fast in accordance with their cycle. Fasting can do wonders for the body as it allows time for the body to repair, restore and heal. When it comes to diet fads, whether it's keto, vegan, or gluten and dairy-free, there's no one-size-fits-all approach. Each of these diets can be effective if followed consistently. However, it's important to focus on a whole foods-based lifestyle, prioritizing vegetables, protein, and mindful carbohydrate consumption. Taking a walk after meals can help mitigate glucose spikes and promote overall energy stability. Processed packaged goods should be avoided, as they often contain additives and unhealthy seed oils. Opting for fresh, natural ingredients is key.

Addressing eating disorders is crucial, both for ourselves and for supporting others. Eating disorders are addictive and challenging to overcome since we must eat to survive. If you or someone you know is struggling with an eating disorder, it's essential to provide support and seek professional help. Limiting entire food groups, such as gluten and dairy, has become a trendy approach to dieting. While some individuals may have legitimate allergies, it's not advisable to create food allergies if you don't have them. Gluten-free and dairy-free alternatives often contain additives and may lack the same nutritional value. Paying attention to how different foods make you feel is essential for healthy, energizing eating. If certain foods feel heavy or cause discomfort, it's best to consume them in moderation or avoid them altogether. It's important to enjoy food without guilt and stress. Eating in moderation and making guilt-free choices is optimal for long-term well-being.

Coffee is a beloved beverage for many, and enjoying it is perfectly fine. However, it's recommended to have a glass of water, preferably with lemon, before consuming coffee. Waiting for an hour and a half after waking up to have coffee allows the caffeine to align with natural energy peaks. Caffeine should be viewed as a tool for energy and alertness rather than a crutch. Savoring a cup of coffee mindfully can be an opportunity for a positive start to the day.

Habit stacking is a powerful technique for incorporating healthy behaviors into our daily routines. By linking new habits with existing ones, we can increase the likelihood of sticking to them. For example, flossing our teeth in the shower or preparing gym attire at night before getting into bed can help establish consistent habits.

Finding an exercise routine that we enjoy is essential for maintaining physical health. Exercise and movement not only support weight management and muscle tone but also contribute to healthy joints, strong bones, improved circulation, digestion, and mental well-being. Engaging in a few minutes of stretching or movement upon waking can have positive effects throughout the day. Sunlight exposure is also crucial for vitamin D synthesis, which plays a vital role in our overall health.

Lastly, it's essential to cultivate gratitude for our health and bodies. Expressing gratitude reminds us of the importance of self-care and taking the necessary steps to maintain our well-being. Nourishing our bodies with proper nutrition, engaging in regular movement and exercise, and prioritizing rest and recovery are all acts of gratitude for our health.

### *Optimal Health 5.1 - alcohol*

Alcohol is ingrained in our society, and it needs to be better understood. The true primary benefit of alcohol is community: people gather around a bottle of wine, celebrate with champagne, or grab beers after work. The important part isn't the drink; it's that connecting with humans is an important aspect of health.

Many of us have made "promises to God" that we will never drink again if this hangover goes away. Let's stop for a moment and realize that we are drinking a beverage that gives us the same symptoms as a low dose of lead poisoning. Alcohol is a strong contributor to weight gain, extremely inflammatory, and lowers your inhibitions. If you think about it in this context, it's probably not a good idea to lower our inhibitions every day or multiple times a week.

Having a drink because you enjoy the taste, similarly to how one enjoys dessert, is different than having a drink to "reduce stress." Alcohol does not reduce stress in the body. I understand that alcohol has a placebo that "takes the edge off," but so do breathing exercises. Don't give your friend not drinking at dinner a hard time. Since alcohol is not going anywhere in the foreseeable future, I will be enjoying a glass of wine or a delicious margarita with you, but let's all, please stop glamorizing blacking out. It is not cool or attractive not to know what you did last night. But I can fill in the blank for you—you wasted money and killed brain cells.

Alcohol damages your organs, and this is particularly bad for your liver and brain. If you care at all about being a high performer, cutting out alcohol will be a great place to start. The analogy I give for alcohol is it's like fast food—you know it's not good for your body, but you may indulge. If you have fast food every day, you will become lethargic and have brain fog. You can probably get away with more fast food while you're young, but it will catch up. All these statements are true for alcohol, except worse. Also, a fun fact: Beer contains phytoestrogen and prolactin. These two chemicals can increase the estrogen levels your body produces. That's why man boobs can be developed; it's ironic beer is quite literally the least manly thing you can consume.

If you consistently crave the feeling of getting drunk as a way to find relief from stress and experience carefreeness. There are healthier alternatives to achieve those states, such as breathwork, meditation, sports, and working out, that can provide similar feelings. Paying attention to our coping mechanisms in life is very important. There are healthy options, and there are unhealthy ones. Every time you choose, you are placing a vote toward what you want in your future. Life is just an accumulation of habits, so you can ask yourself, what are the habits that the best version of myself would do?

# Chapter 6: The Secret Sauce

*"The more tranquil a man becomes, the greater is his success, his influence, his power for good."*

– James Allen

In today's fast-paced world, taking time to care for our mental and emotional well-being is often neglected. However, meditation offers a simple and effective way to cultivate inner peace, improve overall health, and enhance our connection with ourselves and the world around us. Renowned figures like Bill Gates, Will Smith, Jennifer Lopez, Oprah, Ray Dalio, Kendrick Lamar, and Thomas Edison have all spoken about the transformative power of meditation.

One of the most common excuses for not meditating is a lack of time. While it's true that we live busy lives, many successful individuals who juggle multiple responsibilities still find time to meditate. By doing so, we can become the best version of ourselves rather than simply emulating others. If you don't have time to meditate once a day, you are the person who should be meditating twice a day.

Meditation is a gateway to developing a deeper mind-body connection. Just 15 minutes a daily practice can unlock a myriad of benefits. Often, we become drained because we focus solely on external factors, such as work, relationships, or worldly concerns. Redirecting our attention inwards allows us to recharge and tap into a wellspring of energy. The links between stress reduction and meditation are remarkable, and by turning our attention inward, we can experience greater ease and peace in our daily lives.

Getting started with meditation can be as simple as finding guided meditations that resonate with you. Gradually, you can transition to sitting in silence, repeating a mantra, or focusing on your breath. The beauty of meditation is its versatility. It can be practiced anywhere, any time – at home, during your commute, or even on a break at work. You can tap into the benefits of meditation.

Regular meditation practice creates a ripple effect that extends into all aspects of life. It cultivates a state of flow and ease, enabling us to navigate our daily experiences with grace and clarity. This state of flow brings a profound sense of connectedness and oneness with the world. It's a moment where time stands still, and everything else fades away. While some people experience this state during activities aligned with their passions, meditation allows us to access this flow in our everyday lives.

By incorporating meditation into your daily routine, you can reduce anxiety, enhance focus and productivity, and foster a greater sense of well-being. It helps us tap into the beauty and awe of life, experiencing each moment with a renewed sense of presence and connection. As humans, we should actively seek these moments where time seems to dissolve and continually revisit that place of inner stillness and peace.

Meditation is not about striving to become the next Bill Gates or Oprah; it's about nurturing the best version of yourself. Through meditation, you can cultivate self-awareness, inner harmony, and a profound understanding of your true self. Embrace the practice, and let it guide you on a transformative journey of self-discovery and personal growth.

# Chapter 7: Follow-up

*"All of humanity's problems stem from man's inability to sit quietly in a room alone."*

- Blaise Pascal

As we navigate through life as adults seeking happiness and fulfillment, it's inevitable that we encounter unpleasant emotions and experiences. Often, we have the tendency to quickly push these feelings away, especially when we are in situations where expressing them is not appropriate or feasible, such as when taking care of a baby or in the middle of a class. However, it's important to recognize that these feelings will resurface at some point, whether we consciously acknowledge them or not.

When negative feelings arise, it's essential not to suppress them or create narratives to justify them. Instead, take a deep breath and allow the emotion to come up. Recognize it as a feeling, understanding that both positive and negative emotions are natural and part of the human experience. It's crucial not to overreact or over-identify with a particular emotion or feeling.

Feelings and emotions are transient. What once bothered you in the past may not have the same impact now, and vice versa. Instead of allowing your mind to spiral and dwell on past negative experiences, simply observe the feeling as it arises and allow it to pass. If not addressed, these suppressed emotions can lead to disproportionate reactions in various aspects of life. For instance, snapping at a loved one when asked a simple question or displaying unhealthy behaviors like depression, eating disorders, or even personality issues may be expressed.

You may find yourself wondering why certain seemingly minor things trigger strong emotional responses or why someone you know always seems pessimistic. These reactions and coping mechanisms often stem from learned behaviors during early childhood, particularly between the ages of 0-5. Trauma, in this context, refers not only to obvious abuse or neglect but also to situations where our developing brains perceive events as harmful, dangerous, or traumatic.

For example, when you were 3 years old, if your mother picked you up, placed you in a highchair, and then left the room, your young mind may have interpreted this as a threat. Feeling hungry, scared, and alone, your body instinctively entered fight or flight mode. As a young child, your source of comfort and care suddenly disappeared, and you lacked the reasoning abilities or skills to provide for yourself. In response, you cried and screamed, hoping to bring your mother back. The way your parents responded to such situations shaped your understanding of how to get your needs met. If your behavior resulted in your mother returning, you learned that by creating a fuss, you could get what you wanted. This learned response may persist into adulthood, where individuals continue to resort to tantrums or emotional outbursts to manipulate situations. Such behavior is a clear example of allowing the immature impulses of the child's brain to take control.

It's crucial to recognize the profound impact early experiences, and coping mechanisms have on our adult lives. They shape how we respond to situations, the relationships we form, and the patterns we develop. The healing process involves recognizing and acknowledging these triggers and wounds from childhood, as well as addressing and reframing them.

To begin healing, it's beneficial to create a safe and nurturing space where you can explore and process these emotions. This can be done through various methods such as therapy, self-reflection, journaling, or engaging in practices like meditation or mindfulness. By delving into your past experiences, you can gain insight into how they have shaped your responses and behaviors in the present.

Imagine you are 8 years old and have just accomplished something great at school. You're bursting with excitement and can't wait to share your news. However, your parents encounter a flat tire on their way to pick you up, and they are 45 minutes late. Depending on the circumstances and the child, there are two possible reactions. Some children might think, "Great, I get to spend more time with my friends or my teacher!" while others may become upset and fearful because their reliable parent is not there to share their excitement. As a naive 8-year-old, it's challenging to understand that this situation is not a threat and that you will have a chance to share your news later. However, believe it or not, the child who felt hurt and scared during that incident may still carry those emotions within them. These are the individuals who may overreact when someone is just a few minutes late. While it's not wrong to valuc punctuality, if you find yourself excessively upset by cancellations or lateness, it is likely triggering a childhood wound.

Childhood experiences can have both negative and positive impacts on our lives. Tony Robbins, for example, turned his experience of severe physical and mental abuse into the driving force that shaped him into the impressive person he is today. Some of the most successful salespeople or likable individuals you know may have developed their people-pleasing tendencies as a result of a fear of rejection. Similarly, many funny people have honed their skills in entertaining others as a means to cope with the depression or struggles faced by their parents or siblings. These examples demonstrate that childhood experiences can have a wide range of effects on our personalities and behaviors.

Healing your inner child can be immensely beneficial, although not everyone may be ready for it. Keep in mind that you don't actually have to say out loud that you are healing your inner child. You can try it out in your head. Think back to a younger version of yourself. Look at a picture if you need to and see your younger self. Are they upset? What are they upset about? Soothe them in your mind's eye. Hug them, embrace them, and explain to them that you are wiser and more capable. Through experiences and learning, you can take care of them. The 4-year-old version of you or the 16-year-old version of you does not need to be running the show.

When faced with disappointments or cancellations, practice emotional regulation and mature communication. Instead of resorting to pouting or making passive-aggressive comments, express your annoyance in a calm and respectful manner. By doing so, you can handle setbacks and conflicts with a sense of maturity and avoid allowing your inner child to take control.

As you heal your inner child, it's important to recognize that you are no longer that vulnerable child. You have grown, learned, and developed new skills and resources. Allow the adult version of yourself to take the lead in navigating relationships and handling life's challenges. This means responding to situations with maturity, understanding, and effective communication rather than reacting based on old wounds.

Be mindful of patterns that involve creating drama or seeking conflict due to a discomfort with peace and stability. Recognize that healthy relationships don't require constant chaos and conflicts to feel close or secure. Instead, focus on cultivating secure bonds through open communication, trust, and mutual support. Healing your inner child and addressing these patterns will lead to more stable and fulfilling relationships.

As you embark on your healing journey, be patient and gentle with yourself. Healing is not a quick-fix but rather a gradual and on-going process of self-discovery and growth.

# Chapter 8: Exploring Love and Relationships

*"You know you're in love when you can't fall asleep because reality is better than your dreams."*

- Dr. Suess

Love, as a concept, is vast and encompasses a wide range of emotions. It is not limited to a single feeling but holds space for joy, inspiration, anger, annoyance, bliss, fear, and sadness. Love can also be seen as a choice, not an emotion. It is an active decision to continue loving someone despite challenges. It's important to recognize that love extends beyond emotions and can exist even when the object of our love is not present in our lives. Our capacity for love is immense, and what we choose to invest our love in is ever-evolving and changing.

In our society, there is often a disproportionate emphasis on romantic love, which can overshadow the significance of other loving relationships, such as friendships or familial love. Placing romantic love on a pedestal creates unnecessary pressure on those relationships. It is crucial to find ways to give our undivided attention and love to platonic relationships and even strangers. By cultivating love in various relationships, our lives become richer and more fulfilling, which ultimately benefits our romantic relationships as well.

Now, let's dive into some unsolicited dating advice. When it becomes clear that you no longer want to be with someone, it is in both your and their best interest to lovingly end the relationship. Staying in a relationship out of guilt or obligation will not allow either of you to flourish. Dating and relationships can sometimes feel judgmental, but when we quiet our egos and let go of controlling exaggerated ideals, we open ourselves up to the potential of love entering our lives. The individuals who may not love or treat you right should be seen as teaching you how to love yourself.

In a relationship certain levels of commitment are necessary for the relationship to work. Discussing what your ideal life and relationship look like often is an important step. It is necessary to be in alignment and maintain open communication to avoid unnecessary stress. Understanding what the words "I love you" mean to each person involved can help build a solid foundation. While words hold significance, actions carry even more weight. Relationships can be likened to a game of chess, and if the games sound exhausting, remember that you have the choice not to play. However, if you decide to engage in the game, it's crucial to silence your ego and strive to practice unconditional love, which can be challenging.

There's so much attachment but not real love. Conditional love, with its attachments and insecurities, is a natural aspect of being human, but identifying and communicating those conditions is important. Unconditional love, on the other hand, holds no pain because it allows individuals to be themselves without judgment or restrictions. While dating may not be the ideal time to practice unconditional love, gradually moving toward it within romantic relationships can be transformative. Give the benefit of the doubt, but if the doubt persists, make sure it benefits you.

Conditional love can sometimes keep us in the wrong relationships for too long, as we seek fulfillment or validation from the other person instead of finding it within ourselves. It has been observed that when unconditional love forms for oneself and another person within a conditional relationship, the relationship often dissolves peacefully. Unconditional love is more joyful and fulfilling when we tap into it. Even if you have experienced amazing love and lost it, know that the feeling of love resides within you, and it can be found again. Practice unconditional love as much as possible, as it will attract the right people and experiences into your life.

Also, to note, love without trust is practically useless. Not to be dramatic, but trust forms the core pillar of any healthy and meaningful partnership. Without trust, love becomes clouded with doubt, insecurity, and constant questioning. It erodes the very essence of a strong connection, leaving behind a sense of emptiness and uncertainty. Trust is what allows two humans to flourish, enabling vulnerability, intimacy, and mutual support. Without it, love loses its depth and is exhausting.

Whether you are in a relationship or single, there are science-backed ways to maintain the spark. These include activities such as eye gazing, regular physical touch, embracing for more than 3 seconds, laughing together, and engaging in adventurous or novel experiences. These activities stimulate parts of the brain that promote bonding. Do some deliberate learning about your partner. Imagine if you took 45 minutes to have an intentional conversation with your partner about their goals, how they feel, and what makes them excited about life. That experience would be replacing one TV show with something that would literally transform your relationship and bring you much greater levels of clarity and understanding. There are plenty of "swaps" like this one that people can engage in but often don't, which is, in large part, why they don't get what they want. Laziness will never breed an amazing, fulfilling, fun relationship. Choose someone who is aware and accepting of that fact. Investing time in reading relationship books, deliberately learning about your partner, and engaging in intentional conversations can transform your relationship. It's perplexing that we often overlook learning about relationships and communication skills in our education system. Taking the initiative to educate ourselves in these areas can be highly beneficial.

Lastly, it's important not to nag people. Nagging takes up energy and rarely yields positive results. Instead, prioritize constructive communication and finding solutions together. NEVER NAG.

# Chapter 9: Fear is Not Our Friend

*"If you judge a fish on its ability to climb trees, it will forever live its life thinking it's stupid."*

- Apparently, not Einstein

We have all heard the famous phrase, "There is nothing to fear but fear itself." But what does this really mean, and how can we apply it to our daily lives? To put it simply, fear is often worse than the thing we are afraid of. It is the thoughts and emotions we attach to a situation that can cause us the most harm. If you turn on the news, the world is ending, and everything is worse than ever. Well, it turns out if you open newspapers throughout history, that was the same narrative then.

One way to overcome fear is by faking it until you make it. This involves putting on a brave face and acting as if we are not afraid, even when we are. By doing this, we are training our minds to believe that we can handle the situation, and in turn, we become more confident and less afraid.

But how do we start faking it until we make it? One interesting example is by telling others that we are happy. When we tell others that we are happy, we start to self-confirm our own happiness. Our reticular activating system, which is responsible for filtering out unnecessary information and drawing our attention to important things, starts to draw in positive things that confirm our belief of being happy. As a result, we start to become happier.

However, it is important to note that faking it until you make it is not about pretending to be something that you're not. It's about acknowledging your fear and uncertainty while still choosing to take action and move forward with a brave face. It's about telling yourself that you can do it, even when you're not sure you can. And as you start to act and experience small successes, your confidence will grow, and the fear will start to dissipate.

Whenever you face a problem and are feeling fear or having difficult emotions, know that you are human and you are meant to feel. I assure you, no matter what the problem, there are many humans experiencing the same emotion. "Will you ever find love?" "Will you ever be happy?" "Will you ever get over it?" These thoughts feel isolating, but they are actually extremely common. You don’t have to hold your pain in isolation; you can find someone to share it with, whether it is a stranger or a loved one.

There are legitimate moments where you are in danger, but even if you are in a moment of actual harm, fear itself is not going to get you out of it. What we should be fearful of are things that take away our independent thinking: alcohol, indecision, drugs, coercion, and distractions. The brainwashed people force themselves into a small box that God did not create for them, but fear did. Choosing to live in a constant state of worry and fear is creating hell on earth for yourself. We all place unnecessary anxiety and worries on ourselves, our children, and family members in the form of fear, but the less we can do that, the better. Life is an experience, and you get to be the narrator of the experience.

You can train your minds to believe that you are capable and confident and, in turn, overcome your fears. The wise words of Franklin D. Roosevelt, "The only thing we have to fear is fear itself." So go out there and face your fears, one step at a time, and you will find that there is nothing to fear but fear itself.

# Chapter 10: A Note On an Over-Popular Word

*"Reality is merely an illusion, albeit a very persistent one."* - Albert Einstein.

Manifesting, the process of bringing our desires and goals into reality, has been a popular topic in recent years. However, it is often misunderstood as a mystical concept or a shortcut to obtaining desires without effort. In reality, manifesting is founded on the principles of quantum physics and the power of our thoughts and emotions.

Quantum physics is the study of matter and energy at a subatomic level, where one of the key principles states that everything is energy and in constant motion. This means that the vibrations of atoms and molecules, which make up the physical world, can be influenced by our thoughts and emotions.

Manifesting utilizes this understanding by focusing our thoughts and emotions on a specific desire or goal. By aligning our energy with the energy of what we want, we can bring it into our reality. Here are three manifesting techniques that can help align our energy with our desires:

1. Visualization: Visualize a clear and detailed mental image of your desired outcome, incorporating all your senses, and feel as if it is happening now. This practice enhances the power of your manifestation.
2. Affirmations: Repeat positive statements or affirmations that reflect your desires as if they have already happened. By affirming your desires with conviction, you generate a powerful energy that attracts them into your reality. For example, "I am divinely guided. I am met with blessings and abundance every day."

3. Gratitude: Cultivate a sense of gratitude for what you already have in your life. This practice aligns your energy with abundance and positivity, attracting more of it into your life.

In addition to these techniques, it is crucial to be mindful of our daily habits and thoughts. Our thoughts and emotions play a significant role in shaping our reality. By paying attention to our mindset and consciously aligning our energy with our desires, we can manifest the outcomes we seek.

It is important to acknowledge that manifesting is not a magical or instantaneous process. It is a scientific principle rooted in the quantum physics of reality creation. While the term "manifesting" has become overused and even annoying, it serves as a reference point for understanding the power of our thoughts and actions in shaping our lives.

By harnessing the power of our thoughts, emotions, and actions, we can align our energy with our desires and create the life we envision. Manifesting is not about wishful thinking but an intentional and focused alignment of our energy to manifest our desired outcomes in life.

# Chapter 11: Playing the Game - Money

*"Try not to become a man of success, but rather try to become a man of value."*

- Albert Einstein

Money is a game that we all play, and like any game, there are rules and strategies that we can learn to improve our chances of winning. But first, we must understand the psychology of money and how it affects our behavior. People love to hate money, but it's not money itself they should hate; it's other people's ideals. For example, if you want to save the rainforest, having money would make it a lot easier to achieve that goal and raise awareness about it.

One of the key psychological principles of money is that it is a powerful motivator. People often work harder and longer hours when they believe there is a financial reward at the end. However, this motivation can also lead to negative behaviors, such as greed and overspending. In addition, many people are mistaken about the correlation between working hard and making money. Working efficiently, diligently, and thoroughly is a must, but working hard does not guarantee financial success. For example, a waitress at a busy restaurant may work "harder" than a multi-million investment banker, but compensation is not based on physical labor.

Another psychological principle of money is its connection to our sense of self-worth. People equate their financial success with their personal worth, leading to feelings of inadequacy or shame when they are not financially successful. Tying your self-worth to money is not a good choice at all.

Also, accept that you do not win an award for being the most frugal or overpaying for something. It is all relative. If you find it best to always buy on sale, you will feel great about getting a deal. However, determining the true "worth" of an item is subjective.

By recognizing the psychological factors that influence our behavior, we can develop strategies to “loosen our grip on the steering wheel” when it comes to money. Money is one of the easiest and best tools to express yourself, take care of yourself, and be generous. However, there are also many people with more money than they will ever spend who are deeply unhappy. That's why the bigger concepts of self-love, compassion, and gratitude are essential when it comes to money.

As you continue your money journey, realize this about money: it is incredibly personal, and how you spend it, save it, etc., depends on millions of different factors. So, stop wasting your time criticizing how other people spend money. Using your mental energy to evaluate how other people spend money will not make you more money (unless you are considering a consumer investment). A very important piece of advice: do not take financial advice from someone you would not trade bank accounts with. Another important piece of money advice is to date or marry someone who shares a similar financial mindset. Beware of partners who are not grateful for what they have; I assure you that even if they have $500,000,000 in the bank, they will still want more because wanting more is a mindset. And if you are this type of partner, it's time to do some soul-searching because you are setting yourself up for a long, empty life. Money is not the end game; freedom is. Don't get so busy trying to make money that you miss out.

Just like any game, money has certain rules and strategies that we can increase our likelihood of success. By understanding these rules and strategies, we can make better financial decisions and improve our financial situation. Understanding how money works, how to budget, and how to invest it wisely is crucial for a healthy financial life. Without financial literacy, people may make poor financial decisions that can negatively impact their lives. There are four things you should know, have, or understand:

1. Live within your means, no matter how much money you have.

2. You will never get wealthy working a 9-5. It's an important stepping stone in many people's financial journey because it allows you to have money to invest, start a business, or take other financial risks.
3. To accumulate wealth, you must make money while you sleep; find investments that require very little oversight.
4. Understand taxes, assets vs. liabilities, good debt vs. bad debt, and compounding interest.

Not everyone aspires to achieve financial wealth, and that's perfectly acceptable because money alone does not guarantee happiness. However, for those interested in pursuing wealth, it's important to recognize certain key factors. Money is a complex and multifaceted subject, and by comprehending the mental and physical principles that shape our behaviors, one can gain an advantage. A fundamental concept that many fail to grasp is that wealth is intricately tied to consciousness. Even if all the money in the world were evenly distributed, those without money initially would likely find themselves without it again, while those who had money would likely find themselves with more. Money is a mental game, and the adage "the rich get richer" has stood the test of time. This statement doesn't imply that having money automatically ensures its accumulation and growth. Rather, it emphasizes that those with an abundance mindset, who consistently seek and pursue various avenues to generate wealth, are more likely to continue doing so. If one constantly focuses on what things "cost" and perpetually believes there's "never enough," scarcity will persist. While there are different forms of abundance and wealth, if one desires financial wealth, working on personal worthiness, integrity, and a commitment to serving others becomes instrumental in attracting more prosperity. Additionally, acquiring financial literacy is essential for comprehending money matters and making informed decisions regarding it.

When it comes to money, it is important not to judge others based on their financial status. It is essential to recognize that appearances can be deceiving, and material possessions do not determine a person's worth or wisdom. While wealth has historically held power and influence, it is not the sole measure of a person's value. It is a common misconception that individuals with more money are automatically more useful or deserving of attention. While money can be a valuable tool for self-expression on a larger scale, it is crucial to rely on your intuition and discern the truth behind someone's financial facade. Inspiration and breakthroughs can come from unexpected sources, and it is vital to pay attention to people's intentions and ideas. The way you treat those who cannot offer you anything in return is the ultimate reflection of your confidence and character. Money is a game, and by understanding the psychology of money and the principles that influence our behavior, we can navigate the game.

The theory of “mimetic desire” reveals that our possessions often end up possessing us. In the realm of money, social media has exposed us to opulent lifestyles that subtly instill a belief that we need what they have. Unfortunately, this awareness-driven consumption hinders our true aspirations. While accessibility has its merits, our relentless pursuit of luxury can blind us to the invaluable gifts life offers for free. Instead of allowing status symbols to burden us in our quest for freedom and happiness, true fulfillment lies in nurturing our relationships and prioritizing what truly matters. We must acknowledge the sway of marketing and, with discernment, focus on finding lasting contentment by seeking what brings us true joy. The allure of designer possessions may lose its enchantment when we consider that their perceived value does not necessarily align with their actual worth due to credit cards and payment plans.

It is worth acknowledging the changing landscape of accessibility in society, such as everyday conveniences like toilets and services like Uber. These, once considered luxuries, have become commonplace, highlighting the shift in societal perceptions. Instead of doggedly pursuing such trappings, let us recognize that the ultimate display of abundance lies in our ability to care for our loved ones. While I appreciate indulging in luxury myself, I firmly believe that the best things in life are free, and the next best are very expensive. I would be remiss not to mention how overconsumption blinds us to the genuine treasures life bestows upon us without a price tag. Therefore, do not be burdened by status symbols in your pursuit of freedom and happiness. First, find true freedom and happiness within yourself, and then, should you desire, pursue any material possessions that bring you joy. Whether you admit it or not, you have been influenced by marketing, and at this point, marketing belongs next to weather as a force to be reckoned with.

# Chapter 11: Underrated Tools

*"Hard Work will never compensate for lack of alignment."*

- Abraham Hicks

In a world filled with constant trends and advertisements promising happiness and success, it can be overwhelming to determine what choices are truly best for us. With rapid technological advancement and new discoveries being made, it's challenging to keep up with the latest research. So, how do we navigate through this information overload and make the right choices? The answer lies in our intuition. Athletes, entrepreneurs, investors, and mothers alike attribute their defining moments to their intuition. As the world evolves faster than ever, with new devices, research, and analytics bombarding us through marketing and our own desire to improve, it's crucial to rely on our intuition to achieve true life success stories.

Listening to our own intuition is a powerful tool for personal growth and self-discovery. It is our inner knowing or inherent wisdom, and it can guide us through life's challenges. To tap into this wisdom, we must learn to listen to our intuition and trust it. Our intuition stems from our innate wisdom, which is a deep understanding of ourselves and our place in the world. It is not something that can be learned or taught but is inherent within us. When we listen to our intuition, we tap into this inner knowing and allow it to guide us.

One essential aspect of listening to our intuition is recognizing that our body is a brilliant machine. It is designed to safeguard our well-being with the ability to sense and alert us to potential dangers. By tuning in to the signals our body sends us, we can gain valuable insights and make better decisions. Trusting our intuition is also important because it is connected to the wisdom of the universe. Our intuition serves as a direct link to the collective consciousness, providing us with insights and guidance beyond what our rational mind can comprehend.

To cultivate intuition, it's helpful to stop seeking others' opinions on trivial matters like what to wear or what to eat. Instead, ask yourself if you enjoyed something, disliked it, or felt indifferent. Additionally, learning techniques such as muscle testing can be a fascinating way to connect with and develop your intuition. While cultivating intuition may seem esoteric, it's important to understand the practical steps to follow. Once you can hear your own voice and opinions instead of constantly worrying about others' judgment, the next step is discernment. Ideas may come in flashes, but not every idea requires immediate action. Intuitive hits should be coupled with discernment to evaluate their potential. This process requires being optimistically curious, allowing ideas to grow and develop.

Coupled with intuition, delayed gratification and self-control are two highly underrated tools for success. Delayed gratification can be challenging because our brains naturally seek to avoid pain. However, growth often lies within that discomfort. At some point, you must choose between the pain of staying the same and the pain of growth. Having future-oriented goals and a bigger picture in mind can help you make choices that align with your desired growth.

The fastest way to level up is not necessarily what you say yes to but what you say no to. The gaps or lulls mentioned earlier in the book signify periods of reforming and reorganizing. Slow days or months can indicate significant changes on the horizon. Actions should not be solely based on how you feel in the moment. Consistency is key to achieving your goals, regardless of your emotional state. Additionally, if you find yourself in a down wave, it's important not to attach your entire identity to it. Life is constantly evolving, and circumstances will change. Embracing self-discipline and trusting your intuition will make life much easier.

Tapping into your intuition and embracing your inner knowledge is indeed a powerful tool for personal growth and success. Cultivate your intuition by listening to your own voice, paying attention to your body's signals, and being optimistically curious. Coupling intuition with discernment, delayed gratification, and self-control will propel you toward your goals and make the journey more fulfilling. Life is an ever-changing process, and by embracing intuition, you can navigate its complexities with confidence.

# Chapter 12: Cultivating Likability is a Good Idea

*"I'd rather be optimistic and wrong than pessimistic and right."*

-Elon Musk

Being likable is a valuable skill that can greatly enhance our personal and professional lives. People who are likable tend to build strong relationships, achieve success in their careers, and make a positive impact on the world around them. However, it's important to remember that not everyone has to like you, and for the most part, that probably means you're being true to yourself, which is good. Nonetheless, there are certain qualities and behaviors that can make one's personality more appealing with positive energy, and there can be negative energies that can make one's presence dreadful, to the extent that people avoid receiving a phone call. Here are a few ways to be a person others want to be around.

1. Genuinely care and listen: When engaging in conversations, show sincere interest in the other person and actively listen to what they have to say. Demonstrate empathy and understanding, and avoid constantly talking about your own problems or complaining. Being optimistic while still acknowledging reality can also create a positive atmosphere.
2. Follow through on commitments: When you commit to something, make sure to follow through and fulfill your promises. Being reliable and trustworthy builds trust in relationships and enhances your likability.
3. Avoid intimidation or force: Trying to get your way through intimidation or anger may yield short-term results, but it often leads to resentment and pushes people away in the long

run. Allowing others to have autonomy and respecting their opinions and feelings is crucial for maintaining healthy relationships.

4. Focus on building genuine connections: Instead of superficial interactions, strive to build deep and meaningful connections with others. Show genuine interest in their lives, thoughts, and opinions. This genuine connection and mutual understanding will contribute to likability and positive relationships.
5. Communicate effectively: Effective communication involves not only conveying your thoughts clearly but also considering your tone and delivery. Be mindful of how your words and non-verbal cues may be perceived by others. Clear and respectful communication fosters stronger relationships and has a greater impact on those around you.
6. Be authentic and true to yourself: Authenticity is a powerful quality that others can sense and appreciate. By being true to yourself, you create a sense of trust and openness in your

interactions with others and foster deeper connections. Avoid comparing yourself to others, as it hinders authenticity and personal growth.

7. Provide support instead of unsolicited advice: When someone shares a problem with you, resist the urge to immediately offer advice. Instead, ask open-ended questions to help them explore their feelings and thoughts. Be present for them, listen attentively, and allow them to come to their own conclusions. This approach promotes self-discovery and empowers individuals to take ownership of their actions.

By incorporating these principles into your interactions, you can cultivate likability, build genuine connections, and have a positive influence on the people around you. Likability opens doors for new opportunities, as people are more inclined to support and help those they genuinely like

# Chapter 13: Political Discussions at the Dinner Table, Please.

*"To learn, you have to listen. To improve, you have to try."*

- Thomas Jefferson

People hold a multitude of beliefs, and it is common for them to become upset when those beliefs are challenged. This reaction often indicates that many beliefs are adopted without being deeply understood and lived. While every belief begins as an adopted one, the ideal progression is for it to evolve into a lived belief. Through genuine belief and openness to understanding alternative perspectives, we can consider different points of view without compromising our own. This transformative process leads to a knowing; a deep understanding and confidence in our beliefs. With a lived belief, we become less easily offended by opposing opinions because we have a solid foundation of understanding within ourselves. Inner knowing or lived beliefs hold much greater strength.

It is important to recognize that reaching a state of knowing often involves encountering opposition. Therefore, we should refrain from becoming upset when others do not agree with us. Condemning and talking to people will not help us make them see our point of view. To be understood, we must also seek to understand others. This is particularly relevant in the context of politics, where we seem to have strayed from the principles of democracy. We have forgotten that opposing views are an integral part of the democratic process. By demonizing those who hold different political opinions, we demonstrate narrow-mindedness. It is the very existence of disagreement that allows our own beliefs to be options in the first place. Considering the diversity of our world, it is logical that we would hold different beliefs and ideals. In a true democracy, we are meant to bring our ideas to the table, listen to one another, and seek understanding rather than engage in arguments. This way, our beliefs can evolve and become stronger through exposure to opposing viewpoints. Living with a myopic and defensive mindset is stressful and can lead to sleepless nights. It also hinders personal growth by immersing ourselves in confirmation bias.

The current level of polarization in the world is astonishing, and it is clear that some aspects do not add up. Instead of immediately dismissing opposing ideas, it is beneficial to genuinely listen to them. Doing so deepens our understanding of our own beliefs. Ultimately, it is important to let go of rigidly held beliefs and adopt a serene sense of knowing. It is crucial to abandon the roles of solely being a teacher or a student. There are times when we need to be the ones learning instead of assuming we are the ultimate authorities. Plugging our ears and screaming will not benefit us or future generations. It is important to acknowledge that not everyone will acquire the same knowledge in this lifetime, and it is vital to extend grace to others if we are fortunate enough to possess information that brings us closer to feelings of safety, love, and freedom. There is always more to learn, and our understanding is bound to change throughout our lives. If our sole focus is control, it may be worth exploring areas of the world that have adopted communism. Such exploration can foster gratitude and perspective, as there are individuals who would eagerly trade places with us.

Engaging in political discussions with open-mindedness and resilience is vital. It is acceptable to hold strong opinions while remaining open to alternative viewpoints. By striving to understand different perspectives, nurturing lived beliefs, and embracing the principles of democracy, we can cultivate a deeper understanding of ourselves and others. Letting go of the need for control and remaining open to learning contributes to personal growth and a more harmonious society. Our journey of knowledge and understanding is ever-evolving, and by acknowledging this, we can make informed decisions based on what we currently know while remaining receptive to change.

# Chapter 14: How to Stop Holding Yourself Back

*"What we try to hide from always has a way of finding us."*

- Ralph Waldo Emerson

It's inevitable to face various challenges and obstacles in life. During such times, it's common to feel overwhelmed by negative thoughts and emotions and to blame others for our problems. If we aren't blaming others, we are often creating problems through self-sabotage. Self-sabotage is a common issue that hinders us from achieving our goals and living the life we desire. It involves unconsciously undermining our own efforts and preventing ourselves from succeeding. However, by understanding the causes of self-sabotage and learning how to overcome them, we can stop holding ourselves back and reach our full potential.

When it comes to self-sabotage, what are your hiding places? Blame, hypocrisy, arguing, overeating, destructive thought patterns, porn, alcohol, binge-watching TV, doom-scrolling—these are places we turn to when something goes wrong or becomes too good, seeking to hide from the inconvenience of change. Another sneaky hiding place is low expectations. We set low expectations to shield ourselves from disappointment, but it's short-sighted and keeps us stuck in unfulfilling situations. Be aware of your hiding places so you can recognize when they come up and ask yourself why you are choosing something that doesn't move you toward success, love, or abundance.

One of the most crucial aspects of overcoming self-sabotage is the power of positive thinking. Our thoughts profoundly impact our behavior, and by focusing on positive thoughts and beliefs, we can change our mindset and improve our chances of success. It's essential to remain vigilant because self-sabotage often arises when things are better than ever before. It's sneaky and deserves its own chapter in this book. I will delve into more detail about the subconscious mind in the next chapter, but essentially, your mind seeks to keep things the same because it perceives it as safer. For instance, even when you're happier than ever in a new relationship, your mind might say, "Whoa, things havc ncvcr bccn this good before. This is uncomfortable. Let's pick a little fight. I'm used to conflicts in relationships."

Now, let's delve into the concept of self-responsibility. We often tend to blame others for our problems, but the truth is that we hold the key to our own happiness. By taking ownership of our thoughts and actions, we can empower ourselves to bring about positive changes in our lives. Unfortunately, self-responsibility often goes unnoticed and overlooked. Blaming external factors makes you a victim, but you are not a victim. You won the lottery—it's a sheer miracle to be alive. I like to remember the old proverb, "If someone offered to deposit $10 million into your account tonight, but you couldn't wake up tomorrow, would you do it?" The victim mindset leads to dangerous self-sabotage. Many people are unaware that they self-sabotage simply because they are uncomfortable with uncertainty. It's easier to make a familiar bad decision than an unknown good one. With self-responsibility, you consciously make choices that include consciously setting yourself up for positive situations, opportunities, and people in your life. It's evident that people are most triggered when they recognize that they have the potential to do better. The gap between reality and expectation creates stress. We have two options: either bring our reality to the level of our expectations or adjust our expectations to match our reality. (Re-read the last two sentences)

Self-sabotage is a widespread issue that can hinder us from achieving our goals and living the life we desire. By understanding its causes and learning how to overcome them, we can stop holding ourselves back and reach our full potential. Additionally, techniques such as positive affirmations, Emotional Frequency

Technique, visualization, and mindfulness can help rewire our subconscious mind for greater happiness and productivity. The power of positive thinking is crucial in overcoming self-sabotage and reaching our full potential. Because, even though it may be an unpopular opinion, you can have it all. You just need to get your subconscious mind to a place where it believes it, not just your conscious mind.

# Chapter 15: Unlocking the Power of the Subconscious Mind

*"Just as dogs love to chew bones, the mind loves to get its teeth into problems. That's why it does crossword puzzles and builds atom bombs."*

— Eckhart Tolle

The subconscious mind is a powerful and mysterious aspect of our psyche that profoundly influences our thoughts, emotions, and behavior. It is often referred to as the "automatic" or "unconscious" part of our mind, responsible for various processes we take for granted, such as breathing and regulating our heartbeat. However, it also plays a crucial role in shaping our beliefs, actions, and overall mindset. It's important to note that 80 percent of our brain is developed by the age of 3, which means that much of our subconscious programming originates from early childhood, which can explain some of our childish or inconsistent behaviors.

One critical understanding of the subconscious mind is its immense power compared to the conscious mind. It drives the majority of our thoughts, beliefs, and actions, making it challenging to change these patterns through conscious effort alone.

To tap into and utilize the power of the subconscious mind, we need to employ techniques that bypass the conscious mind and directly access the subconscious. Visualization, affirmations, hypnosis, and mindfulness are some of the most effective methods for reprogramming the subconscious mind and transforming limiting beliefs. By utilizing these techniques, we can work towards achieving our goals, improving our mental and emotional well-being, and evolving into our best selves.

Another critical aspect of the subconscious mind lies in its influence on our emotional life. Our emotions are closely intertwined with the subconscious, and it can be challenging to manage and regulate our emotions when they are connected to unconscious thought patterns. However, by understanding the subconscious mind's role in our emotional experiences and employing techniques like visualization, affirmations, and mindfulness, we can gain greater control over our emotions and enhance our emotional well-being.

When you consciously strive to reach the next level of success but seem to encounter obstacles or self-sabotaging behaviors, it's often because your subconscious perceives it as a threat. While many individuals rise through the ranks without consciously addressing their subconscious, having an understanding of how it works can help address miscommunication or potential roadblocks more efficiently. Without this awareness, there is a risk of unintentionally derailing your progress in various aspects of life, whether it's making poor business decisions or jeopardizing relationships.

Have you ever wondered why things are going well in a relationship, only for sudden fights to erupt?

Or why do you struggle to perform after landing your dream client? Perhaps you have a brilliant idea but can't seem to find the time to execute it. These experiences stem from your subconscious mind's response to unfamiliar territory. It's as if your subconscious is saying, "Stop, wait! We've never experienced this level of love, success, money, or happiness. It's scary. Let's sabotage it to stay safe." While it may sound irrational, the subconscious mind's primary concern is your safety, and anything unfamiliar, even if it appears better, can be perceived as a threat. Emotional Frequency Technique (EFT) can be a useful tool to facilitate breakthroughs in such situations. Additionally, ask yourself, "What could go wrong if I achieve [insert desired outcome]?" and allowing time for thoughts and emotions to surface can reveal underlying fears and concerns. Common responses include worries about losing relationships, not fitting in with friends, or facing potential judgment. It may sound unbelievable, but this is a real phenomenon. Consider your dream life and then observe what doesn't match your current reality. That disparity represents the extent to which you have subconscious work to do.

Understanding and unlocking the power of the subconscious mind is paramount for personal growth and success. By employing techniques like visualization, affirmations, hypnosis, dream journaling, and mindfulness, we can gain insight into our subconscious programming and reshape limiting beliefs. This process leads to enhanced mental and emotional well-being, improved relationships, and the ability to achieve our goals. The subconscious mind holds the key to unlocking our full potential, and by harnessing its power, we can take control of our lives and create the future we desire.

# Chapter 16: Building Healthy and Fulfilling Relationships

*"When we love, we always strive to become better than we are. When we strive to become better than we are, everything around us becomes better too."*

- Paulo Coelho

People are an essential part of our lives, and the relationships we cultivate can profoundly impact our well-being, happiness, and success. Whether they are family members, friends, romantic partners, or colleagues, the people in our lives shape our identity and influence how we perceive the world.

Nurturing healthy relationships is crucial for our overall happiness and well-being. To foster healthy relationships, effective communication, setting clear boundaries, honesty, and willingness to compromise are essential. It is also important to cultivate forgiveness and be open to asking for forgiveness. Additionally, being receptive to feedback and demonstrating a willingness to change when necessary is crucial for fostering growth within the relationship.

Serving others is another significant aspect of building strong relationships. By prioritizing the needs of others above our own, we can establish deeper connections and find a sense of purpose and fulfillment in our lives. Serving others can take various forms, including volunteering in the community or offering support to a friend in need.

Appreciation is key in relationships, but it's important to acknowledge that life is short. Therefore, we should appreciate people for who they are at the present moment. It is essential to recognize that individuals can only help themselves if they consciously engage in personal growth and self-awareness. Attempting to save someone who is not ready for change can harm our well-being. Another valuable tip in navigating relationships is observing who someone's friends are and the duration of those friendships. This insight can provide significant information about a person, as we are influenced by those we spend the most time with.

A renowned Harvard study, unique in its examination of human lives across socioeconomic backgrounds and age groups, highlights two key factors that contribute to a happy life: the quality of relationships and self-care. This study encompasses various aspects of life, such as finances, education, marriages, and children. The findings indicate that individuals with happier lives prioritize nurturing healthy relationships and taking care of their bodies. Notably, the study reveals that these two factors are interconnected, as individuals with better relationships tend to exhibit healthier habits such as consistent sleep schedules, reduced alcohol consumption, and regular doctor visits. It is crucial to recognize the significance of this study, as it removes victimhood and ego from the equation and succinctly demonstrates that fostering healthy relationships and practicing self-care

are essential for a happy life. While happiness may not be the sole goal for everyone, prioritizing these two aspects can significantly impact overall well-being. Moreover, the study suggests that stress management is significant, as both healthy relationships and self-care contribute to lower stress levels. This, in turn, can result in reduced inflammation and improved physical health. The book also offers a range of stress management tools for individuals who currently lack healthy relationships or struggling with unhealthy habits.

Honesty is a critical component of fostering great relationships. Reflecting on promises unkept and lies told is important to address underlying guilt and negative projections that may be affecting our lives. It is crucial to understand the reasons behind these actions and, with love, release them while seeking to correct our course. Lying not only hurts others but also damages our own self-perception. It reinforces the belief that we are wrong, bad, or inadequate. Practicing self-acceptance allows others to show surprising levels of acceptance as well. Holding onto lies or further entrenching them can lead to anxiety, headaches, or even contribute to autoimmune issues. Even seemingly harmless "white lies" ultimately have detrimental effects, as upholding false ideas never proves beneficial in the long run.

Avoiding criticism and blame is another key aspect of cultivating strong relationships. Criticism is generally unpleasant, particularly in professional or personal relationships. Before criticizing someone, it is valuable to pause, take a deep breath, and reflect on a time when we made the same mistake and faced criticism. Choosing compassion or offering suggestions instead of criticism can significantly improve relationships. If there is one habit from this book to apply to your life, refraining from criticism will bring about tremendous positive change. Initially, it may be challenging to suppress feelings of frustration, but with time, these emotions will dissipate.

While it is common knowledge to avoid spending time with negative individuals, it is equally important to be mindful of those constantly engulfed in fear. Financial markets have historically fluctuated, and unfortunate events have always occurred. Surrounding ourselves with individuals fixated on society's problems reinforces a sense of helplessness and fear. It is crucial to be aware of this dynamic and seek positive and empowering relationships instead.

Overall, the people in our lives significantly influence our experiences and personal growth. The Harvard study underscores the profound impact of relationships on our well-being, showing that having a loving partner can even contribute to better physical health and faster recovery from illness. Building healthy relationships and serving others are crucial elements for our happiness and overall well-being. By improving our communication skills, setting boundaries, being honest, and willingness to compromise, we can foster strong relationships that support and sustain us throughout our lives. It is vital to recognize the power of the people in our lives and to invest in nurturing these relationships, as they can contribute to a life filled with love, connection, and meaning.

# Chapter 17: The Metaphysical Body

*"Listen to the Whispers so You Don't Have to Hear the Screams."*

- Elizabeth Gilbert

The metaphysical body encompasses the interconnectedness of our physical, emotional, and spiritual well-being. It acknowledges that our physical bodies store memories and experiences, including trauma, which can manifest as physical symptoms and emotional distress. When faced with moments of self-doubt or overwhelming emotions, it is important to allow ourselves to fully experience and process these feelings.

Instead of suppressing or overriding negative emotions, take a deep breath and let the emotion come up without judgment or the need to justify it. Recognize that both positive and negative emotions are a natural part of life, and it is unrealistic to expect a constant state of positivity. Overreacting or overly identifying with a single emotion can lead to unhealthy patterns. Emotions and feelings change over time, and what might have bothered you in the past may not affect you in the same way now.

It is common to believe that our pain is unique or exceptional, but in reality, experiencing pain is a fundamental aspect of being human. The specific circumstances and reasons behind our pain may be unique, but the experience of emotional pain is shared by many. How we respond, react, grow, love, and treat others in the face of adversity truly sets us apart. Embracing our emotions and learning to process them allows us to avoid having them reflected back to us in destructive ways.

Anger, for example, does not have to manifest as breaking things or yelling at people. It is possible to gaslight ourselves out of acknowledging anger, as I have personally experienced. By denying my own anger, I inadvertently attracted angry people into my life. It wasn't until I recognized and accepted my own anger that I felt a sense of relief. Anger can take various forms, and sometimes it may simply feel like acceptance. Allowing ourselves to feel a range of emotions, both dark and light, is essential. It doesn't have to be a dramatic outward display but rather a space where emotions can be acknowledged, honored, and given the breadth they deserve.

Since trauma can become ingrained in the body, it is crucial to address both the physical and emotional symptoms that arise from it. Various modalities can be used to heal and bring balance to the metaphysical body. Practices such as yoga help release tension and emotions stored in the body, promoting relaxation and healing. Bodywork therapies like massage, craniosacral therapy, and somatic experiences can also aid in releasing stored tension and emotions, facilitating healing. Acupuncture is another modality that balances the body's energy and promotes overall well-being.

Furthermore, mind-body therapies like meditation and mindfulness can help release emotional and psychological components of trauma. By listening to our bodies and giving space to our emotions without resistance, judgment, or moralizing, we allow for healing and create a more harmonious connection between our physical, emotional, and spiritual selves.

To summarize, the metaphysical body recognizes the interconnectedness of our physical, emotional, and spiritual well-being. It is important to address both the physical and emotional aspects of trauma. By attuning to our bodies and respecting our emotions, we can embark on a transformative healing journey. Our bodies provide honest messengers, and it is crucial to heed their signals and listen attentively to them.

# Chapter 18: The Pain of Staying The Same vs. The Pain of Growing

*"Every new beginning comes from some other beginnings end."*

- Seneca, the Elder

The adage "no pain, no gain" is frequently used to depict the journey of self-growth and personal development. It suggests that growth and transformation can be challenging and accompanied by discomfort, but ultimately, the reward outweighs the costs. However, this is not always the case. In fact, the pain of staying in a situation that is not serving us can be much worse than the pain of growing and changing.

When we stay in a situation that is not healthy for us, we not only miss out on the potential for growth and change, but we are also exposing ourselves to ongoing pain and suffering. For example, while leaving a toxic relationship may be difficult and painful in the short term, it can ultimately lead to healing and growth. On the other hand, the pain of growing and changing is often temporary and, over time, leads to long-term benefits. For example, pushing ourselves out of our comfort zone to try new things can be scary and uncomfortable, but it leads to increased self-confidence and personal growth.

Developing confidence and nurturing self-growth can be a challenging process, but there are several effective strategies that can assist us along the way. Feeling a lack of confidence is actually just that you are confident in your own doubt. One of the most important things to not lose sight of is to be kind and compassionate towards ourselves. We are all human, and it is normal to make mistakes and experience setbacks. By being kind and compassionate towards ourselves, we can develop self-acceptance and resilience. Another important strategy for developing confidence and supporting ourselves in self-growth is to set small and achievable goals. By setting small and achievable goals, we can build momentum and confidence, which will help us to tackle bigger challenges in the future. It is also essential to surround ourselves with supportive people. Having a supportive network of friends and family who believe in us, and encourage us to grow and change, can be incredibly powerful. These people can provide emotional support, encouragement, and practical help when we need it most.

The pain of staying in a situation that is not serving us can be much worse than the pain of growing and changing. While change and growth can be uncomfortable and difficult, the long-term benefits are worth it. Developing confidence and supporting ourselves in self-growth can be challenging, but by being kind and compassionate towards ourselves, setting small and achievable goals, and surrounding ourselves with supportive people, we can overcome the pain of staying and embracing the pain of growing.

# Chapter 19: Be Grateful if You're Thankful

*"Those who don't believe in magic will never find it."*

- Roald Dahl

Gratitude is the practice of being thankful for the things we have in our lives. It is a powerful tool that can profoundly impact our well-being and happiness. By developing a gratitude practice, we can improve our mental and emotional health, build stronger relationships, and create a more positive outlook on life. It can be easy to take the good things in our lives for granted, but by actively cultivating a sense of gratitude, we can shift our perspective and find joy in the present moment. By taking time each day to reflect on what we are grateful for, we can train our minds to focus on the positive and experience a greater sense of well-being.

If you are already one of my daily gratitude list people, I would like to point out a fatal mistake I and others have made. It is when we find ourselves in a challenging relational or work situation, and we try to say we are simply not being grateful or strong enough. I have, of course, tested this out for you: "If I can just be stronger, less bothered, and more grateful, this situation will work." No, don't waste your time. Go to the chapter on cultivating your intuition. You're not going to be "grateful" for your way out of a toxic friendship or work environment.

One of the most powerful effects of gratitude is that it helps us shift our focus from what we lack to what we have. When we are focused on what we lack, we often feel unhappy and dissatisfied with our lives. However, when we focus on what we have, we are able to appreciate the good things in our lives and find contentment.

Gratitude can also help improve our mental and emotional health. Studies have shown that people who practice gratitude have lower levels of depression and anxiety and are generally happier and more satisfied with their lives. Additionally, gratitude can improve our physical health by reducing stress, strengthening the immune system, and improving sleep.

Another benefit of gratitude is that it helps us build stronger relationships. When we are grateful for the people in our lives, we are more likely to appreciate and value them. Additionally, expressing our gratitude to others can strengthen our connections and build deeper, more meaningful relationships. There is nothing worse than an ungrateful person. Romantic and friendly relationships fizzle when you forget to be thankful for the little things.

Let's bring back the power of gratitude. Often, we overlook the incredible gifts we have, such as the miraculous functioning of our bodies. Inside us, thousands of processes work tirelessly to keep us alive effortlessly and without conscious effort. It's easy to take these marvels for granted. If you ever find it hard to think of something to be grateful for, consider the boundless supply of oxygen that fills our lungs, allowing us to breathe and thrive. Reflect on the importance of even the simplest body parts, like our big toe, which provides balance and stability. By acknowledging these blessings, we can reignite a sense of appreciation for the extraordinary aspects of our existence.

Developing a gratitude practice can be approached in various ways. One simple method involves writing down three things you're thankful for each day. A supercharged way is to write down three things you are currently grateful for and two things you want but do not have, as if you already have them. Another approach involves genuinely expressing your gratitude to someone in your life, whether that be a friend, family member, or colleague. You can also start a gratitude jar, where you write down things you are grateful for and put them in a jar. You can go back and read them when you need a boost. The most important part of a gratitude practice is to feel gratitude. Place your hand on your heart and say what you are thankful for.

# Chapter 20: Cultivating Happiness

*"If you want others to be happy, practice compassion. If you want to be happy, practice compassion."*

- Dalai Lama

In a world that often emphasizes personal gain and self-centeredness, the practice of altruism and compassion stands as a powerful antidote to the pursuit of happiness. Altruistic thinking involves prioritizing the needs of others above our own, which may initially seem counterintuitive in a society that encourages us to focus on our own desires. However, research has shown that acts of selflessness bring about a profound sense of fulfillment and contentment that cannot be attained through selfish pursuits alone.

One way to incorporate altruistic thinking into our lives is by engaging in simple acts of kindness. Holding the door open for someone, offering a genuine compliment, or extending a helping hand can significantly impact both the recipient and ourselves. These acts not only brighten someone else's day but also foster a sense of connection and purpose within us. Engaging in volunteer work or community service is another meaningful way to make a positive difference in the lives of others and contribute to the well-being of our communities.

Cultivating happiness as a skill also involves being intentional with our thoughts and actions. It is easy to get caught up in negativity, focusing on the challenges and hardships we encounter. However, by consciously redirecting our attention towards the positive aspects of life, we can train our minds to see the good even in difficult situations. Engaging in the practice of gratitude and positive thinking has the potential to cultivate a more optimistic and joyful outlook, enhancing our overall well-being.

It is important to recognize that altruistic thinking and cultivating happiness as a skill require consistent practice and dedication. They are not one-time actions but ongoing commitments. However, the effort invested in these practices is immensely rewarding, as the benefits of living a life centered around the well-being of others and ourselves are immeasurable.

Altruism also provides a profound counterbalance to depression, often resulting from a sense of meaninglessness in life. By embracing altruism, we discover that a fulfilling life is built upon caring for others, pursuing passions, mentoring, and showing kindness to both friends and strangers. By recognizing the interconnectedness of all beings and understanding that our actions have a ripple effect, we can contribute to the well-being of all. Every act of kindness and compassion, no matter how small, carries significance and can create a positive impact on the world around us.

In a society that often equates happiness with the acquisition of material possessions and the pursuit of personal desires, it is important to challenge this notion. While external markers of success may bring temporary pleasure, true well-being, and lasting happiness are found in selflessness and acts of kindness toward others. Giving rather than receiving brings a sense of fulfillment and purpose that surpasses any material gain.

Personal experiences often highlight the limitations of material pursuits in providing lasting happiness. The realization that acquiring external markers of success does not guarantee fulfillment is a transformative insight. Instead, practicing altruism and focusing on the welfare of others bring genuine and enduring happiness.

If you are ready to embark on a journey toward a fulfilled life, I encourage you to shift your focus away from yourself and embrace acts of altruism. Instead of dwelling on self-pity, make it a daily practice to perform acts of kindness, no matter how small. Preparing your partner's favorite beverage, cleaning up a mess you didn't create, or assisting your neighbor with their tasks can profoundly affect not only your well-being but also on creating a ripple effect of goodness. Small acts of thoughtfulness toward others will bring more positivity into your life than you can imagine.

By practicing acts of kindness, prioritizing the needs of others, and consciously redirecting our thoughts toward the positive, we can cultivate genuine happiness. Happiness and fulfillment are not found in personal achievements alone but in our ability to bring joy and well-being to others and ourselves.

# Chapter 21: The Meaning of Life and Finding Your Purpose

*"Life has no meaning. Each of us has meaning, and we bring it to life. It is a waste to be asking the question when you are the answer."*

— Joseph Campbell

The question of the "meaning of life" has intrigued philosophers and thinkers throughout history. While different perspectives exist, finding your purpose can bring a sense of fulfillment and satisfaction to your life, regardless of whether life has an inherent meaning or not.

One way to begin the journey of discovering your purpose is by exploring your passions and interests. What activities or subjects genuinely excite and inspire you? What are you naturally drawn to? Your passions and interests often provide valuable clues about your purpose in life.

Additionally, it is essential to reflect on your unique strengths and talents. What are you naturally good at? What skills and abilities come effortlessly to you? By identifying and utilizing your strengths, you can make a meaningful contribution to the world and experience fulfillment in your endeavors.

Considering the impact you want to make and the legacy you wish to leave can also help you find your purpose. What values and causes are important to you? How do you aspire to make a difference in the world? Identifying a purpose that aligns with your values and transcends your individual self can provide a profound sense of meaning and direction.

It's important to recognize that the search for purpose is a lifelong journey, often characterized by trial and error. It may involve experimenting with different paths until you find what truly resonates with you. Embrace the process, and do not be afraid to make mistakes or explore new possibilities.

Life's meaning undergoes transformation akin to the changing seasons, mirroring the cycles of nature. Each phase presents its own unique experiences, whether it be growth, chaos, love, or lack. These experiences can manifest in various aspects of life, such as relationships, careers, travel, or hobbies. Understand that these aspects will change and evolve over time.

Trusting in a bigger picture and having faith in a higher power or plan can provide solace during uncertain times. Personally, I find comfort in the belief that I am divinely guided and that the universe is working in my favor. Even in challenging situations, I strive to learn, love, and grow while viewing every experience as an opportunity for personal development.

The meaning of life is a complex and personal question, and the search for purpose is an ongoing journey. Rather than worrying, surrender to where you are in the present moment. Embrace the changes, trust in the process, and allow yourself to evolve as you navigate through life. Your purpose may unfold in unexpected ways, and every experience contributes to your growth and understanding of the world.

# Chapter 22: Playing Big

*"Do you want to know who you are? Don't ask. Act! Action will delineate and define you."*

- Thomas Jefferson.

Taking risks and stepping out of your comfort zone is essential to living a fulfilling life. Many people regret not taking more chances and pursuing their dreams when looking back on their lives. However, it's never too late to start "playing big" and embracing the power of risk-taking.

One crucial aspect of playing big is recognizing that you are the main character of your own life. You have the ability to shape your reality and determine your own destiny. Take ownership of your own life and make choices that align with your goals and aspirations. Refrain from placing the responsibility for change solely on external factors, as it is crucial to maintain agency and actively pursue the life you desire.

Playing big doesn't always mean taking enormous risks. It can involve starting small by trying new things, speaking up, or taking incremental steps outside of your comfort zone. The key is to be true to yourself and pursue what you genuinely desire, even if it feels challenging or unfamiliar.

Overcoming the fear of failure is an essential element of playing big. Failure is a natural part of the learning process and provides an opportunity for growth. Embrace failure as a chance to learn and improve, allowing it to motivate you rather than hold you back. Every failure brings valuable lessons that can propel you forward on your journey.

It is crucial to detach yourself from the opinions of others, especially those from your past. The judgment of people you went to high school with or others who may not understand your aspirations should not deter you from pursuing your dreams. You are the main character, and their opinions are merely supporting roles in your life's narrative. Focus on your own growth and fulfillment.

Playing big is about taking risks, stepping out of your comfort zone, and pursuing your dreams. It's never too late to start living the life you want and embracing the possibilities that lie ahead. While it's important to have a sense of urgency, it's also wise to have a plan and prepare before making drastic changes. Assess your situation and have certain things in place before taking significant leaps.

Life may be more mysterious and dynamic than we initially perceive. Embrace the unknown, level up, and go after what you want. Whether it's wearing a certain outfit, going on a trip, starting a side hustle, or simply betting on yourself, playing big is about taking intentional action and pushing the boundaries of your comfort zone. Trust in your own potential, and never underestimate the power of stepping outside of what is familiar and safe.

# Chapter 23: The Power of Non-Judgment: Embracing Acceptance

*"Serenity comes when you trade expectations for acceptance."*

-Gautama Buddha

Non-judgment is a powerful practice that can greatly enhance one's life. It entails letting go of criticism and embracing acceptance, both for ourselves and for others. By adopting a non-judgmental mindset, we can cultivate understanding, compassion, and positive growth.

One fundamental principle of non-judgment is recognizing that everything is happening for our

circumstances appear
s often a higher purpose
ng in the journey and
ı reason behind every
ife with acceptance and

˙ the need to control or
ɪnt and criticism. Trying
ior or actions through
le because we cannot
can focus on our own
ɪrovement. By releasing
d focusing on ourselves,
we create a space for personal development and positive change.

When we encounter individuals who exhibit judgmental and controlling behaviors, it can be helpful to recognize that their actions are often rooted in their own insecurities. Rather than condemning them, we can empathize with their struggles and redirect our attention to our own internal wounds and insecurities. By examining our own reactions and understanding why we feel defensive or critical, we can gain insight into our own areas for growth and healing.

Non-judgment also extends to accepting ourselves as we are and letting go of comparisons to others. Each individual's journey is distinct, and comparing ourselves to others only diminishes our own self-worth and prevents us from fully embracing our own potential. By accepting ourselves for who we are and celebrating our own unique path, we can foster self-love and inner peace. Additionally, incorporating novelty into our non-judgment practice can bring beauty and freshness to our relationships. Instead of constantly comparing the present to the past or seeking perfection, we can cultivate a sense of intrigue and appreciation for change.

Embracing novelty and letting go of criticism and judgment creates space for growth, understanding, and deeper connections. Practicing non-judgment is an ongoing journey that requires patience and self-compassion. Breaking the cycle of judgment and insecurity starts with embracing self-acceptance and extending that acceptance to others. By practicing non-judgment, we create a more loving, accepting, and compassionate world.

# Chapter 24: Practicing Non-Resistance; A Skill For Ultra-Successful Humans

*"When you struggle against this moment, you are struggling against the entire universe."*

-Deepak Chopra

Practicing non-resistance is a shortcut to finding inner peace and transforming our outer circumstances. It involves letting go of the need to control or change things and instead allowing them to unfold naturally. By embracing acceptance, trusting in the journey, and releasing attachment to outcomes, we open ourselves to a profound greater sense of peace and create positive transformations in our lives.

One of the key aspects of non-resistance is recognizing that our reactions and emotions are within our own control. When we feel angry or upset towards someone, it is not the other person causing those emotions, but rather our own attachment or resistance to the situation. By becoming curious about our feelings and exploring the underlying reasons for our reactions, we can gain insight into ourselves and find ways to release resistance.

Letting go of attachment to outcomes is an important aspect of non-resistance. Often, we become fixated on specific outcomes and feel frustrated or upset when things don't go as planned. By relinquishing our attachment to outcomes and surrendering to the natural flow of life, we can find peace within ourselves and allow things to unfold as they are meant to. This includes not manipulating situations or relationships to achieve desired responses but instead allowing genuine and authentic outcomes to emerge.

Trusting in the journey is essential in practicing non-resistance. It means understanding that life is a series of experiences, lessons, and growth opportunities. We can truly enjoy the journey by shifting our focus from solely chasing the destination to wholeheartedly appreciating the present moment and the lessons it holds. Embracing change and uncertainty is also a vital aspect of non-resistance. Life is inherently unpredictable, and resisting change or clinging to certainty can lead to suffering and dissatisfaction. By accepting and embracing change, we can gracefully navigate transitions and adapt to new circumstances. Understanding that everything is temporary, including our own lives, can help us appreciate the preciousness of each moment and live more fully.

Practicing non-resistance is an ongoing journey that requires patience and self-reflection. Reprogramming our minds involves releasing control and resistance, surrendering to the natural flow of life. By cultivating acceptance, trust, and resilience, we can find inner peace and create positive transformations in our outer circumstances. Non-resistance does not mean being passive or complacent. It is about finding inner harmony and responding to life's challenges with grace and openness.

# Chapter 25: Quiet the Critic

*"Never be overheard complaining, not even to yourself."*

- Marcus Aurelius

Self-criticism is a common habit that can have detrimental effects on our well-being. Understanding the science behind self-criticism can help us break free from this destructive cycle and embrace radical self-acceptance and wholeness.

Research in cognitive psychology has revealed that self-criticism activates the same neural pathways as physical pain. This suggests that self-criticism can be incredibly distressing and challenging to let go of. Moreover, self-criticism often stems from a belief that we are inadequate or unworthy as we are, perpetuating a narrative of self-hatred.

The narrative of self-hatred is pervasive in our society, causing many people to constantly feel inadequate and miserable. However, the truth is that we are all inherently worthy and complete, just as we are. Embracing radical self-acceptance means letting go of the belief that we need to be different or better to be worthy. It involves acknowledging and celebrating our inherent wholeness.

Practicing self-compassion is a powerful way to release self-criticism and foster self-acceptance. Self-compassion involves treating ourselves with kindness, understanding, and forgiveness, just as we would treat a friend. It means not judging ourselves harshly for our mistakes and imperfections. It's important to realize that everyone is shaped by their environment and experiences, and compassion can help us understand the root causes of negative behavior in others without condoning it. Extending kindness to ourselves and others can be transformative and healing.

Reframing our thoughts is another effective strategy for overcoming self-criticism. When negative, self-critical thoughts arise, we can consciously reframe them by focusing on our strengths, accomplishments, and positive aspects of ourselves. By deliberately shifting our perspective, we can reinforce a more positive and compassionate view of ourselves. It's worth noting that understanding the reasons behind our self-critical tendencies can be helpful. Still, it's also essential to avoid getting stuck in a never-ending quest for self-analysis. A way to practice compassion is before you speak and ask yourself, "Is it Kind?" and "Is it Truthful?" If the thought or question passes those two questions, then carry on. If not, skip it.

Practicing self-acceptance and self-compassion is a continual process. It requires patience, self-reflection, and a commitment to nurturing a kind and loving relationship with ourselves. By embracing our wholeness, letting go of self-criticism, and cultivating self-compassion, we can experience profound transformation and live a more fulfilling and joyful life.

# Chapter 26: Loneliness

*"Loneliness expresses the pain of being alone, and solitude expresses the glory of being alone."*

-Paul Tillich

Loneliness is a prevalent issue in today's society, despite the fact that we are more connected than ever before. It's important to understand that loneliness is not solely about physical proximity or the number of people around us. Rather, it stems from a deep-seated need to be seen, understood, and valued for who we truly are.

Studies have shown that loneliness can affect individuals even when they are in relationships or surrounded by people. This is because true connection requires a deeper level of understanding and emotional resonance. Loneliness is a complex and multifaceted feeling that can be incredibly dangerous, leading some individuals to contemplate or act upon suicidal thoughts. If you or someone you know is experiencing mental health issues, it is crucial to seek help from professionals trained in addressing suicidal thoughts and behaviors. One lesson that can never be talked about enough is how impermanent every single thing is. No matter how bad the season is, it is not permanent. Loneliness is a scary season in life to face. It is an urgent concern, so consider this now. As you go throughout your day, how could you help people around you feel seen?

To combat loneliness, it's essential to cultivate authentic connections with people who genuinely support and love us. It's important to be discerning in choosing who to be vulnerable with, as criticism and doubt can hinder our ability to be ourselves. Surrounding ourselves with positive and supportive individuals who understand and appreciate us is key to combating loneliness.

While spending time alone can be beneficial, it's important to recognize that physical human connection holds significance from a psychobiological perspective. Engaging in activities that involve physical touch, such as hugging or holding hands, can have numerous benefits. However, it's equally important to ensure that our interactions with others are positive and uplifting, as negative human interaction can be detrimental to our well-being.

Finding non-judgmental spaces, either in person or online, can provide a sense of community and understanding. Joining philanthropic organizations or participating in online support groups can connect us with like-minded individuals who share similar experiences and perspectives. Feeling seen and understood by others who resonate with us can help alleviate the feelings of loneliness. Expressing love and appreciation to the supportive people in our lives is also important. Regularly reaching out to those who uplift us and letting them know that we value and love them strengthens our connections and reinforces a sense of belonging.

At a broader level, it's crucial to recognize that the increasing prevalence of loneliness may be linked to our societal tendency to numb ourselves with distractions and to neglect self-reflection. Existence is only tolerable for so long before people choose to escape it with some vice. Happiness is saved for the weekends…. patterns of dissatisfaction are accepted. However, finding ways to reconnect with ourselves and savor the simple pleasures in life is essential. Taking the time to stay present in moments of joy, compassion, and love can help combat the patterns of dissatisfaction and bring more fulfillment to our lives. The next time you see a touching moment, one that sparks real joy or compassion, try to stay in that moment longer. Believe it or not, we have to get comfortable staying in pleasure. We have all of these complex lofty goals that we perseverate on, but we overlook simple moments of joy. You are after that big goal of being happy, right? So why are you skipping over the pockets of joy already available to you? The beauty of life lies in the little pockets of love that occur daily, such as watching a sunrise, observing a mother caring for her baby, or witnessing a random act of kindness. These seemingly small moments carry immense power and should never be overlooked.

You are resilient, loved, and the world needs your authentic version. By prioritizing genuine connections, seeking supportive environments, and embracing moments of joy, we can work towards combating loneliness and cultivating a sense of belonging and fulfillment in our lives.

# Chapter 27: The Interconnectedness of Life

## *Embracing the Quantum Web of Connection*

*"Realize that everything connects to everything else."*

– Leonardo DaVinci

The concept of quantum entanglement in physics teaches us that particles can be interconnected in a profound way, where the state of one particle is intertwined with the form of another, regardless of distance. This principle also extends to our lives and relationships, offering a profound understanding of the interconnected nature of our existence.

To grasp the quantum entanglement of life, it is crucial to recognize that our thoughts and actions reverberate and have a ripple effect on those around us. The energy and vibrations we emit influence the people we interact with; reciprocally, they impact us. This understanding empowers us to realize the profound influence we have on the world. It allows us to consciously choose to focus on positivity and love, thereby creating a positive difference.

The field of physics, particularly quantum mechanics and the study of high-energy subatomic particles, has shed light on the significance of frequencies in the occurrence of particles and events. Surprisingly, scientific research has unveiled frequencies that transcend the confines of space and time. Through advanced mathematical analysis, it has been observed that the human brain perceives and interprets these frequency patterns. These discoveries have led to theories proposing the universe's holographic nature, suggesting an intricate interconnectedness of all things. This implies that each individual is intricately linked to the entire cosmos, and our consciousness plays a pivotal role in shaping our realities. Exploring the relationship between consciousness and the fabric of reality continues to evolve. Expert David Pike from the University of London explains that our brains construct reality by mathematically decoding these frequencies, unveiling a realm of meaningful patterns that transcend time and space. Thus, our brains can be seen as operating in a holographic manner, perceiving and engaging with a multidimensional reality.

The profound understanding of the quantum entanglement of life urges us to acknowledge our interconnectedness and interdependence. We exist within a vast web of relationships, and our choices and behaviors have profound effects not only on ourselves but also on those around us. By embracing this interconnectedness, we can strive to live in harmony with others, making decisions that consider the well-being of the collective.

One practical application of this principle in our lives is cultivating an optimistic mindset and attitude. When we hold positive thoughts and radiate high vibrations, we elevate the energy of those around us, fostering a more positive and harmonious environment. Additionally, by choosing compassion and empathy in our actions, we foster positive connections and relationships with others, contributing to a more harmonious world.

The quantum entanglement of life reveals the profound interconnectedness of all things. By acknowledging the extension of our thoughts and actions beyond ourselves and recognizing our integral role within the greater whole, we can live with a deeper sense of responsibility and unity. Let us embrace this understanding and strive to create a world where love, compassion, and harmony flourish.

# Chapter 28: Your Journey - The Power of Subjective Truth

*"You don't have the truth. You have your truth."*

-Ric Elias

In our subjective experience of reality, we hold our own truths. It's a powerful realization that our happiness, love, and fulfillment are not dependent on external factors but are inside jobs. Achieving external goals may not always lead to lasting happiness, as it is our perception and interpretation that determines our level of excitement and satisfaction.

The uniqueness of each individual becomes evident when we consider how different people can have contrasting desires and preferences. What excites and fulfills one person may not have the same effect on another. Our individuality and intuition significantly guide us toward our goals and align us with what truly resonates with our authentic selves.

Sometimes, we need to experience a sense of underlying misery to recognize that something is not meant for us. It's important to pay attention to the signs and feelings that arise when we are not aligned with our purpose. There are certain levels of individuality and intuition in what I believe is God's perfect plan that also leads us in certain directions. Recognizing this allows us to learn valuable lessons and remain open to new opportunities while cultivating inner peace along the journey.

The journey itself is where growth and transformation occur. Goals and aspirations serve as valuable guides, yet it is the process of pursuing them that offers the most profound experiences and lessons. As we strive for success, power, fame, or financial abundance, we discover that the fulfillment we seek lies not solely in achieving those external markers but in the personal growth, self-discovery, and connection with others that come with the journey.

While on this journey, it's essential not to take ourselves too seriously. We must let go of self-imposed rules and expectations, embracing the freedom to explore, adapt, and evolve. Appreciating the diversity of approaches and perspectives allows us to learn from others and celebrate their unique journeys alongside our own.

Life is a tapestry of experiences, and it is through contrast that we appreciate the value of both positive and negative aspects. Wanting, longing, and experiencing various feelings are inherent to our human existence. Embracing the full spectrum of emotions without fear of potential hurt or rejection expands our capacity for love, compassion, and growth.

Letting go of the need to label, categorize, and classify opens up a world of possibilities. Life is not black and white but rich with shades of gray. Embracing complexity and change allows us to navigate the ever-evolving nature of our experiences with greater ease and openness. If you had everything you ever wanted from the beginning of your days, you wouldn't know what wanting is, so you wouldn't know the value of what you have.

Ultimately, the true winner in life is the person who finds contentment, self-love, and love for others. Through personal growth, evolving perspectives, and embracing the journey, we cultivate a sense of fulfillment and make the most of our human experience.

As you continue on your unique journey, stay open, adaptable, and compassionate. Embrace the gray areas, embrace change, and let your subjective truth guide you toward a life filled with growth, love, and fulfillment.

| IN | OUT |
| --- | --- |
| Acupuncture | Nagging others |
| Gratitude | Being nagged |
| Altruism | Victim mindset |
| Grounding | Scarcity mindset |
| Journaling | Lack of Boundaries |
| Sleep Hygiene | Oversharing |
| NSDR | Seed oils |
| Reading | Procrastinating |
| Breathwork | Alcohol |
| Physical touch | Weed |
| Compassion | Gossiping |
| Self-discipline | Hook Up Culture |
| Honesty | Inconsistency |
| The sun | Vaping (obviously) |
| Individuality | Ignoring intuition |
| Dopamine Detox | Overstimulation |

Made in the USA
Middletown, DE
14 September 2023

38543655R00087